CELL YOU
A THEORY

a study of life

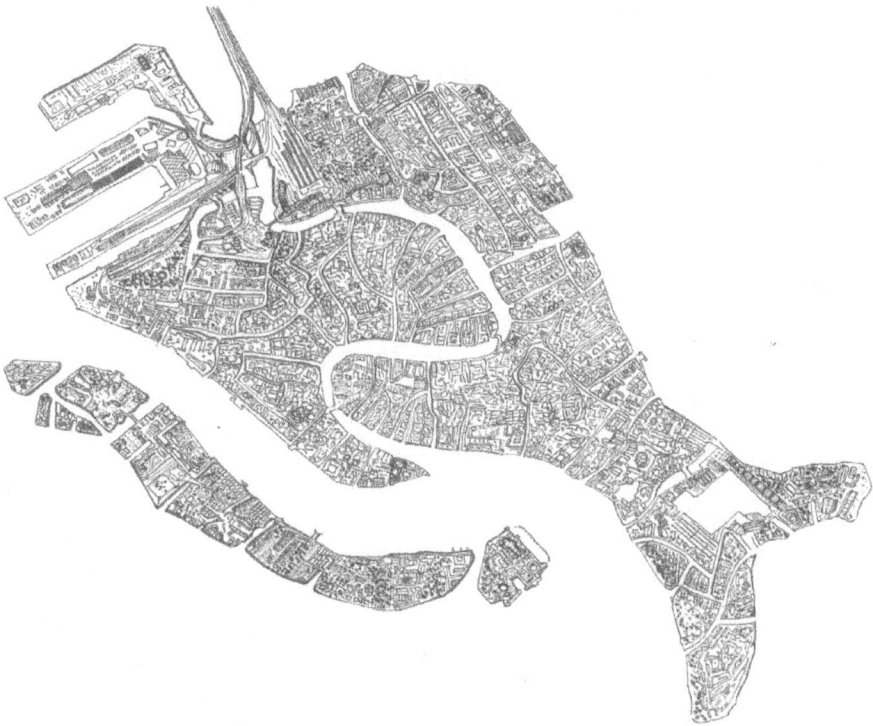

DR. HARKI DHILLON
MD. FRCS, Msc Orth.

ISBN-13: 978-0578403793(HiCARE Inc.)

ISBN-10: 057840379X

CELL YOU A THEORY
A study of life

HARKI DHILLON
MD, FRCS, MSc ORTH

The cover of the book is a satellite view of Venice, Italy. This image was chosen because it encompasses a lot of what is written in this book. There is water all around this island with a central canal and multiple smaller canals. Densely packed on this island and 'fed' by canals, are houses with humans.

This man-made environment can very easily represent a multicellular organism (A fish) with a gastrointestinal canal, arteries and densely packed and organized cells.

INDEX

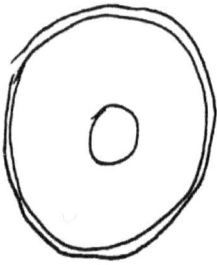

Cell

Human Being
30-100 trillion cells

PREFACE

For the last four years, every time I looked at any living thing, I wondered about the little guy / gal - the cell. This book is my journey into the microcosm of the cell and my interpretation of single cells, multicellularity, the human organism and much more.

In conversations with people in these last four years I have seen that the subject of this book is a complete mystery to them and is not thought about or discussed by most people, ever! We are so familiar with life that we see all around us and the shape that it has taken that we take it for granted and don't feel the need to go deeper. On the other hand, I am fascinated by the fact that cells have been around for billions of years, resilient, productive and organized.

There is a connection between the cell and the human race. Our behavior is controlled by a formula which I think exists and I have attempted to explain it in this book.

Acknowledgements.

I would like to thank Avika Dhillon for designing the cover and Aman Mann, Rimmy Mann, Rakesh Kelkar, Rajiv Anand and Deepta Dhillon for reviewing the manuscript.

INTRODUCTION

I have studied the human form for forty years in all its wondrous dimensions – from cell structure and function, conception and embryology to the development of this beautifully designed Human Being that functions like a well – oiled machine except that this 'machine' has LIFE. It has movement, thoughts and feelings and a definite life span. Things can and do go wrong due to disease and trauma quite often resulting in early death. Each body encases within it an indomitable spirit and a will to accomplish dramatic and awe-inspiring feats.

I have been involved at a personal and clinical level in the process of birth and death, of illness and recovery and as a surgeon, having performed thousands of surgeries, looking at who and what we are, from the 'inside'. I have listened to hearts with a normal reassuring beat and rhythm and to the abnormal diastolic and systolic murmurs, felt the pulse with dropped and irregular beats revealing a system in distress. I have listened to the benign, normal sounds of air entering and leaving the lungs but also to the sounds of lungs drowning in fluid in congestive heart failure and distressing sounds of wheezing in asthma. I have listened to normal bowel sounds but also to fluid tinkling in ileus or paralysis of the gut. I have cut open patients and seen beautiful, normal tissue and ugly, abnormal, diseased tissue – what I think of as nature's beauty gone wrong. I have put my patients back together, cured them and relieved them of their pain. I have seen cells in section in their stained beauty and unstained nakedness.

I have lived and worked on three continents and treated people of all ages, colors, races and religions. They all bleed and heal, feel the pain of illness and disease, the joy of recovery and health and the grief of loss and death.

The path taken to become a doctor is long and arduous and begins in High school and Pre-med, with the study in significant detail of Biology (Botany and Zoology), physics, chemistry and mathematics.

I learnt plant and animal cell structure, cell metabolism and function. I studied the Amoeba, the Paramecium, the fruit and the flower, the cockroach, the earthworm, the frog and the rabbit – study that included the meticulous drawing of the Hibiscus rosa-sinesis, shading in the beauty of the stamens, the petal and the sepals and then dissecting the rabbit and studying the circulatory system, the digestive, reproductive and other systems.

Forty years ago, for the first time, I had a patient in the operating room under anesthesia. I cut into live tissue but did not see the millions of cells the blade went through, as blood spurted with the pulse of life. Over the years I have 'been into' the brain, the spine, the liver, the bowel, the kidneys, muscles and joints – treating injury, infection, cancer, degenerative disease and much, much more.

So, I have looked at the beauty of life, the ugliness of disease and the stillness of

death and from the preserved cadaver revealing its details to the warm corpse hiding its mystery.

Then one day death touched me in the form of a heart attack and I nearly lost my life. Survival provided a strong stimulus to think about this unique phenomenon called LIFE.

It is not only Science that is important to the study of life. History took me through the rise and fall of civilizations, their blossoming and dying like fields of flowers, battles and wars, periods of peace and prosperity, mighty conquerors and cruel dictators, the systems of democracy and communism – essentially the complexity of human interaction. We study Geography that helps us to understand the land masses, ocean
and wind currents, to know more about the planet we live on.

Science and mathematics attempted to analyze the Universe, the cosmos and the galaxies – so we could build rockets and spaceships to explore and colonize planets.

This intimate journey has brought out many introspective moments when thoughts of what life is and how and why we came to be, why we do what we do in this circle of life and what ultimately is the formula that reveals to us the secrets that give us the answers to the mysteries of our existence. These thoughts are explored through science, religion, philosophy and our limitless imagination.

I hope this will encourage constructive thought and discussion to further propagate the search for answers we would all like to know.

INTROSPECTION.

If I was the first person to sit back and think who we humans were and I did not have the luxury of drawing upon a base of scientific knowledge – what would my thought process have been, say, a 100,000 years ago?

I sat cross legged in a cave. It overlooked a wide expanse of land bathed in the waning light of the setting sun. I saw some of my people returning from a foraging and hunting excursion. Lately I had started spending more time thinking about who 'my people' (we) were and where we had come from. I felt I was different from the rock that I was leaning against – that I had something vital. I was alive. This life that I had was similar to what the squirrel, the bird and the scorpion had. The squirrel in front of me also had a nose and two eyes, two arms holding a nut which it nibbled on.

There were so many living things that moved, walked, ran, flew and swam. They had mates and babies. There were plants that grew and had flowers and fruit and had baby plants.

But I had seen some of my people lose their lives, lose that vital force that kept them doing things which helped them live and survive only to die from illness, injury and old age. When I saw dead bodies of people and animals, I noticed that they did not breathe, the chest and belly did not move, and they did not mist a shiny surface that was held close to their nose and mouth.

 I did not want to die. This thought itself was confusing because I did not know why I did

not want to die. I tried to hold my breath, but something in me – life- would not let me. I had to breathe to live, till the time illness and age would naturally end my life. I knew that with each breath I took I stayed alive. I also knew that I could not stay in one spot for very long. I had to find water to drink and food to eat. Life made me do it.

I knew that there was a natural end to life, but I knew that It, life, 'wanted' to go on – rejuvenated with new and young bodies and that was why I felt the urgent, powerful need to mate so I could contribute to this process called life.

I did all that I could to protect myself and my family so life would not disappear and, yet we had a choice. If we did not mate and

produce babies' human life would cease to exist. Why had we been given this choice? Did all other animals have a choice or was it a pre-ordained function?

I did not know that a hundred thousand years (many, many cycles of the seasons) from now there would be science and art and religion that would open doors to point us in directions that may shed light and knowledge about the who, what and why of life.

It just seemed to be the way things were. Life began and ended, but with each passing year I saw our numbers increase.

LIFE

Life is our greatest 'gift'.

We are 7.5 billion people in the world are leading a complex interactive life. Each person is made up of 30 - 100 trillion cells with another 35 trillion cells in the gut.
Very few people think about who 'we' are, how we came to be and where we are going. {Why don't we?} - so I did a survey composed of nearly equal males and females, aged 18 to 65 years, education was high school, some college, MDs and PhD. Questions were asked and a written response was given.

A summary of their response is provided. {Reader - try and answer these questions and see if you agree with summary of their response.} The questions were:

Define Life.

When did life start and how?

When did Human Beings appear on earth?

What is a Human Being?

Number of cells in the Human Body.

What is the most significant
achievement of the Human Being?

The summary of each question/answer -

Define Life: -
Life is a journey,
- a gift to be cherished and enjoyed with
a need to procreate,
 -have children and to nurture them.
-Life has an end.
-Life is a biological and biochemical
process in harmony.
- It can breathe, taste, smell and talk. -
It is 'being alive'.

When did life start and how: -

-"No one knows when life started" but estimates from this group were -
at the Big Bang,
-4.5 billion years,
-10 million years,
-50 million years and
-50 thousand years.
-Life starts at birth.
- Many did not think about it at all.
-Only one response was - By God.

When did Human Beings appear on earth.-
-Most respondents had never thought about it and other guesses were from
-10,000 years,
-50,000 years,
-1 million and

-5 million years ago.

What is a Human Being? -
  A Human Being is a person,
-not an animal, thing or object,
-the most complex of mammals, over
and above the animal kingdom with a
superior intelligence and a moral
compass.
  -A human being is a lover, teacher,
student, a monster.
-A human being has an ability to
perceive feelings with a brain to analyze
and make things happen.

Number of cells in the Human Body: -
  All respondents of this survey knew
that the body had cells but then there

was a huge difference in the number of
cells they thought made up the body. It
varied from
10,000,
30 million,
80 million,
100 million,
1 billion,
4 quadrillion and
infinity (forever reproducing).

Most significant achievement of the
Human Being: -
 -Is having a child,
-being born,
-to reproduce,
-finding and giving love,
to save lives,

-to understand the human body,

-to treat and cure ailments.

-To create knowledge, ideas, thoughts
that helps society progress,

-to prolong life,

-to take away pain.

-Humans 'self-study',

- to learn how we act and react to
situations,

-maintained existence and survived,

- have self-consciousness and morality.

-The development of medical
knowledge and lower down in degree of
achievement - the internet and fire.

Science helps us study ourselves and
our past. But - studying our behavior

tells us a lot about where we are headed and that is what this book is about.

The passage and expanse of time is very important to keep in mind as we look at the history of life and the future.

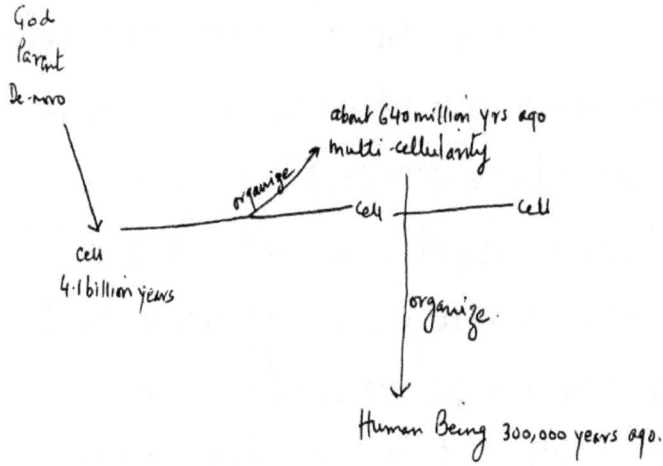

God
Parent
De-novo

about 640 million yrs ago
multi-cellularity

organize

Cell   Cell

Cell
4.1 billion years

organize

Human Being 300,000 years ago.

LIFE.   Chronology.

There appears to be a lot of scientific documentation and investigation to establish when water first appeared on earth. Earth itself was born 4.6 billion years ago, single cell life appeared 4.1 billion years ago with water probably present earlier. Earliest oxygen was at 3.56 billion years followed by photosynthesis at 2.5 billion years. From 2.5 billion years to 1.5 billion years is the age of Eukaryotes (cells that contain organelles in the cytoplasm, a membrane bound nucleus with genetic material and a system of division by mitosis/ meiosis). Multicellular life appeared – 640 million years ago.

We of course would not exist if the single cell life form would have continued as it had been doing for billions of years.

The question is whether the single cell population organized itself to become more efficient as the next logical sequence or it was already programmed in the genetic makeup of life to go from a single cell gestational phase to the multicellular form of life.

We do not know why life came about but there is speculation and multiple theories on how it may have happened. We will explore some of these now and come back to the formation of the multicellular organism and relate it to what happened 300,000 years ago and then again about 10,000 years ago.

THE PRIMORDIAL SOUP THEORY. In early earth simple organic compounds were produced due to the atmosphere and energy. These compounds accumulated in a 'soup' which may have been concentrated at various locations (shore lines, oceanic vents etc.). Further transformation formed more complex organic polymers, and ultimately, life developed in the soup. The Muller-Urey experiment, much quoted used a highly reduced mixture of gases – methane, ammonia, hydrogen to form basic organic monomers such as amino acids.

The question is whether life originated by accident or there was Divine intervention of life 'injected' into receptive material.

HYDROTHERMAL VENT THEORY. A hydrothermal vent is a fissure in the planet's surface from which geothermally heated water comes. There are extreme conditions of heat and pressure. There is no sunlight, so chemicals are used for energy. Scientists have also traced DNA of all currently living organisms back to a common ancestor extremophile that would have been formed in the hydrothermal vents.

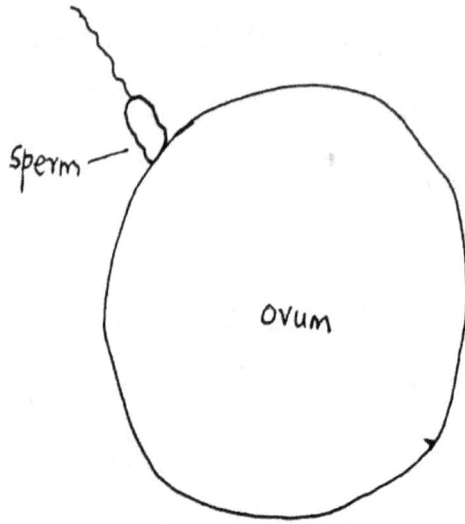

Sperm

Ovum

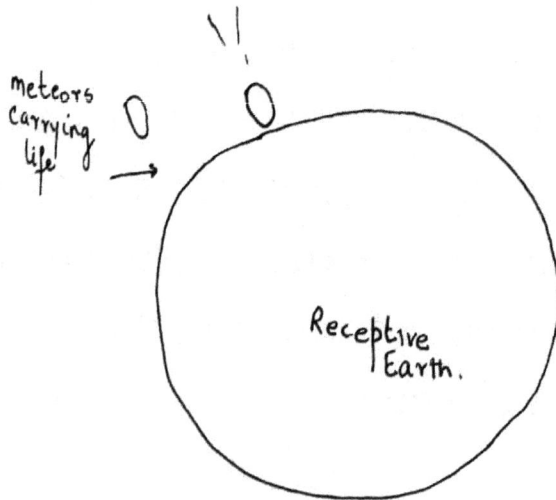

meteors
carrying
life

Receptive
Earth.

Theory of Panspermia

PANSPERMIA 'SEEDS EVERYWHERE' THEORY. This was first mentioned by Greek philosopher Anaxagoras {Philosophy involves rational inquiry into areas that are outside of either theology or science}, around 500 BC. 'Seeds' were dispersed everywhere from outer space and most likely came from meteor impacts.

In the late 1700's Benoit de Maillet talked about - 'seeds being rained down to the oceans from the Heavens'.

In 1800's Lord Kelvin suggested life came with 'stones' from another world.

Francis Crick talked about "Directed panspermia'.

Amino acids are common on meteors today.

I find the use of the word seed or seeding interesting, in that life may have arisen, as, in the humans where sperm penetrates a receptive egg resulting in life. Seeding indicates that life came to this planet and found receptive conditions to further propagate. It took billions of years for single cells to start forming multicellular organisms e.g. The Human Being, who appeared in this present form 300,000 years ago from Primary areas of origin on the planet and has spread to all corners of the globe and now attempting to spread even further to other planets OR we might be the Primary mass arising de novo and spreading OR we might be a secondary focus coming from elsewhere. Primary and secondary are terms that describe the kinds of cancer.

One of the ways cancer kills is by disturbing or destroying resources by interfering with the blood supply and by taking up nutrients which are required by 'normal' tissue. The human race at this stage is interfering with the planet e.g., deforestation, pollution, excessive waste and many other ways. Unchecked growth and spread will help in our own extinction – cancer kills itself by killing the host.

Of all the celestial (cell-estial) bodies It may have been that Earth was receptive to the seeding and formation of life.

A proliferation of humans in a big city 'destroys' 'nature' and looks like a cancer in the body

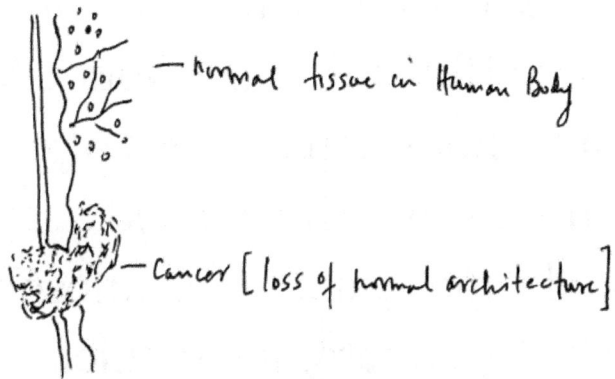

— normal tissue in Human Body

— Cancer [loss of normal architecture]

As primitive cellular existence took hold – the air and vapor stayed- possibly related to its weight, the velocity of the planet in its orbit (67,000 miles per hour) and its rotation on its axis (1000 miles per hour). Metabolism of trillions and trillions of cells over billions of years created a layer of air and vapor called the atmosphere. This blanket, micrometers thick, covered the planet which became warmer on the surface by trapping the heat, like a nursery, this environment facilitated progression of life. This cushion of air worked like a cell membrane/ wall. {A tree absorbs 48 pounds of carbon- dioxide per year and produces 260 pounds of oxygen per year. One human being uses 55 liters of pure oxygen per day.}

CANCER

Theories of meteorites bearing life would fit this scenario and would not rule out life on any 'receptive' world. This then takes me into another concept – alluded to earlier, that we behave like a cancer where we have metastasized from a primary focus elsewhere and having established this 'secondary' site of the metastatic process on earth and are now working diligently to spread to a tertiary site – Moon, Mars and beyond.

Cancer (Malignancy) is a word that we fear because it describes a phenomenon that kills. That itself makes us probably not relate to being a cancer but there are enough similarities of how we behave and how cancer behaves that it is worth looking at it.

Malignant cells grow from any tissue. Cancer is characterized by growing and spreading to other parts of the body (metastases).

God
Parent | life
De-novo |

[Specialized cells. One type may have been] 'cancer' cells'

multicellularity

Cell ——————— Cell

Cell

Human Being

- About 40% of men and women will be diagnosed with cancer at some point in their lifetimes
- Some studies show 50%.

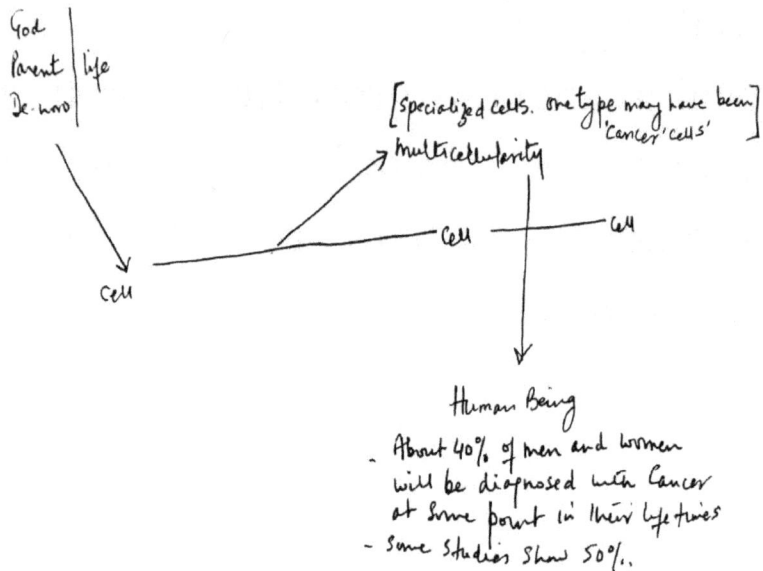

There is a main or Primary growth and a Secondary growth resulting from the metastases. Cancer that grows slowly has cells that have more or less normal architecture (well differentiated) and rapidly growing cells, spreading early, shows loss of normal cellular architecture (Anaplasia).

 It is not difficult to imagine that during the billions of years single cells existed there
was some variation in cell metabolism, cell growth and cell division which created cells that passed on their characteristics to future generations and these cells also were incorporated into the multicellular organisms (MCO) then these would present with 'abnormalities' which could be classified as cancer because they had the ability to spread/metastasize.

Throughout this book the example of the multicellular organism (MCO) is the Human Being.

 In the body cancer develops and spreads and in a similar manner in which Humans behave. They get together in a place, organize to survive in an efficient manner e.g. making a township – drastically changing the characteristics of the local region and then 'spreading'- making similar towns and cities. A histological section of a cancer specimen under a microscope looks like a satellite picture of a town and its normal surrounding area. Cancer growth and spread has been classified into stages. Stage 0 is 'in-situ' or still in place where it started, stage 1 only spread a little into nearby tissues, stage 2 and 3 has spread into nearby tissues and lymph nodes and stage 4 into other parts of the body.

Human beings on the planet may be 'local infiltration' or stage 3 as we are everywhere on the planet and we would be considered stage 4 if we colonized mars or the moon.

Our aim is always to discover cancer in the body as early as possible for treatment to be successful but getting it identified at stage 1 or 0 is not common even though the 'cancer' cells may always have been there. On the other hand, stage 3-4 can causes enough symptoms to initiate a search to diagnose and start treatment. In most patients we do tend to find the cancerous lesions and then methods of treatment are put into motion – e.g., surgery, excision, amputation, chemotherapy, radiation therapy etc. These can have significant side effects. If treatment is not successful, then death follows with the end of the human and its cancer. At this time, on the planet, humans are manifesting stage 1 to 3 but when we get to stage 4 then we might attract the attention of our 'parent' who might institute a radical form of treatment to eradicate us or it might then be too late, and we will kill the host – our planet. This may take hundreds of thousands of years or billions of years. A malignancy in the human body goes its course in 6 months, 6 years, 16 years or more depending on degree of aggressiveness of the tumor and intensity of the treatment.

Spacecraft have been sent into space as probes to study and 'check out' the environment, to see if there is life out there or if some planet would be suitable for life which would help us decide to move to that planet, inhabit it, utilize resources and repeat the pattern. Our behavior may help us understand how a malignancy behaves in our body. Does cancer in our body send out cells or parts of the cancer cell into the circulation looking for a receptive area in the body which provides access and nourishment to these scouting malignant cells where there may be lack of defending normal cells, and so establish a secondary lesion? These messages (of having found a good place to settle) are carried back by malignant cells or cell products to the parent body which then releases cells to travel to recommended areas and take hold to form a colony.

Within the 'well differentiated' organized Human Being presence on earth there is generally a common goal - peaceful co-existence, to flourish as the human race. Within this mass of humanity there has arisen in recent times the specter of terrorism – which helps a certain section of humans to take over by spreading fear by aggressive, life threatening methods to spread their own ideology. Certain 'human cell nests' attempt to take over much bigger cell groups to control life in a manner of their choosing. As they (the terrorists) spread from one area to another they are commonly referred to as being 'metastatic'. The Human Race may behave as a cancer and 'terrorists' can be an aggressive cancer within a cancer.

RELIGION

There are theories of Life based on what Science has given us, but people/humans have believed in a Creator for thousands of years and the majority of the human race follows some religion – (the belief in and worship of a superior controlling power.) The question remains why without scientific evidence the majority of the 7.4 billion people believe in a God. Is it possible we have information in the life code within us that gives us a sense of where and what we come from and that we are built in the image of our creator (the Ultimate Parent) just as we have babies who grow into adults and look and behave like their parents?

I have put together a basic outline of what certain religions believe on the concept of the origin of life.

CHRISTIANITY: 2.4 billion or 33% of the world's population is Christian and the religion is 2018 years old. In this religion the belief is that God created the world in six days and rested on the seventh day.

"In the beginning God created the Heavens and the Earth," and importantly, - "So God created Man in his own image: male and female He created them."

HINDUISM: This, the oldest religion, is a collective term applied to many religious and philosophical traditions from India. There is no specific moment of origin or a Founder. The tradition considers itself to be timeless, having always existed. It probably dates back five to seven thousand years and has about 870 million followers. Lord Brahma is the creator of the Universes and the first in the triumvirate. The other two are Vishnu, who sustains creation and Shiva, the destroyer of evil. Though the belief in one supreme God is common, Hindu texts consider all deities to be extension of this god. The three gods form the supreme one who is behind all creation and destruction. These gods create and destroy universes continuously. (death of cells within the body?). Time for this process is unaccountable. One day for Brahma is considered 4 billion years for man. Brahma creates all life, all distinct and different species come from different parts of the Brahma's body. The creation tradition in Hinduism is not clear.

The soul is the common vital entity in every living being.

SIKHS: 30 million people are adherents of this faith and it has been around for 550 years. Guru Nanak, the founder of Sikhism said – God is the creator of the

Universe and of Life in all its
manifestations.

The true Lord created the air,
From Air, water arose
From water, creation arose
His light permeates all creation.

Guru Nanak considers the Human Body
a vehicle for the soul. The body is
called the Temple of God. Sikh gurus
generally accepted the traditional view
of 8 million and 400,000 species of
living organisms in the Universe.

The Shri Guru Granth Sahib (Holy
Book) says there are 42,00,000 species
that exist in water and the same number
exist on land.

The aim of our life, according to the
Sikh Gurus is to develop the best in us -

which is God. This could be a reference to recognize that the human was developed in the image of God.

BUDDHISM: this religion started 2551 years ago and has about 500 million followers.
'The origins of beings revolving in Samsara (Life Cycle) being cloaked by Airjja (ignorance) is undiscoverable'.

ISLAM: (1.7 billion followers). Founded in the 7th century. The Quran does not offer a single unified theory regarding the Creation of the Universe and how life began on earth. The Quran also states that Human life began with Adam and Eve in the Garden of Eden –

a belief shared by Christians and Jewish faiths. I believe that this may have occurred when single cells which had been developing for billions of years became multicellular, with many species being formed, the human, being one of them and were formed as male and female. The Garden of Eden may be a place which provides an environment which may have been suitable for the formation of this particular (Human) multicellular organism just as earth proved to be suitable for the development of life and the single cell organism.

The Quran says, "the heavens and the earth were joined together as one unit, before we clove them asunder". (The beginning of the Universe).

ATHEISM: 592 million followers. Documented in the 18th century and now are 8% of the world's population. Atheists have an absence of belief in the existence of deities.

Origin of life for atheists is related to abiogenesis which is the natural process by which life arises from non-living matter such as simple organic compounds.

There are other ancient forgotten polytheistic and monotheistic religions which have their own belief systems on life and creation.

Out of 7.4 billion (the world's population) 6 billion follow some religion and these are the people who believe in the Creator or Deities who created the Universe and Life and the millions of species of plants and animals.

The question is whether 'Life' carries a message within us that makes us believe in a 'Greater Life' or the Creator/God. Does a newly born baby know it has come from the womb or that it has a mother or father?

Even if we do not believe in the initiation of life from the Divine or a Creator, the unavoidable fact is that life exists and has done, according to the scientific world, for 4.1 billion years.

The atoms, molecules, amino acids etc., formed life and had code built in (DNA) that probably did direct how life would perform and what it had to do to survive. It took life 3.6 billion years to evolve into the human being.

Survival does seem to be a very powerful force for any living thing. It is not easy to describe life, but intuitively we know life when we see it. It is indescribably beautiful and vital. It is easier to describe its absence – the loss of color, the loss of tone and elasticity, the absolute stillness and total loss of all that is vital. Something we call Death.

All life dies – it deteriorates to the end point – of death. Yet it keeps going – restarting the clock with birth.

An extremely important aspect of one's existence is the concept of time. Human beings have quantified (long/short) time and qualify (good/bad) time, measured it in hours, minutes, seconds, nanoseconds and years but have not been able to give it a satisfactory definition.

I think of Time as a unit of deterioration. A Human is born and then dies, at an average age of 80 years. Ants live from a few weeks to many years. Common garden birds live 2 to 5 years and cells in the human body live from a few days to the life time of the human but ultimately all will die. Even the sun will 'die'.

Radioactivity is measured by its 'half-life'- that is the time it takes for half of the atoms of the radioactive material to disintegrate. It could be a few microseconds to billions of years. How much time will it take for anything animate or inanimate to deteriorate? The only way to 'stop time' is to create. Creation initiates the start of time, but deterioration begins in that instant.

LIFE CHARACTERISTICS

Most people when asked to define life find it very hard to do so but attempts have been made to do this and there are certain characteristics of life that should be considered. Life needs –

-Organization,

-metabolism,

-homeostasis: this is the mechanism by which the body maintains optimal conditions for efficient functioning e.g.., maintaining normal Blood Pressure, temperature, Blood sugar, electrolytes etc., with organs (collection of specialized cells) interacting and working together.

-Growth,

-reproduction (sexual, asexual),
-response and evolution.
Organization: When life began or 'arrived' it had to ensure that it had the ability to use available nutrients to sustain itself with the process of metabolism (anabolism and catabolism). Anabolism is the synthesis of complex molecules in living organisms from simpler ones together with the storage of energy and catabolism is the breakdown of complex molecules to form simpler ones. For the sake of efficiency and protection against the elements, life needed a cell membrane in animals and a cell wall in plants to become active and carry out the functions mentioned above.

{Organelles contained within a cell wall is the basic unit of life}.

Organization also brought cells together to form multicellular organisms. Evidence of earliest life was 4.1 billion years ago, and evidence of earliest water was before that, maybe a few hundred million years, which indicates that life probably grew in or around water and as oxygen became more plentiful, life forms adapted away from water but also continued in water.

A central thesis of this book is that we may get answers of what life does and how it may have done it, is by observing and studying what 'we' do, 'we' being prime examples of life on earth at this this time. Lessons are to be learnt by finding connections between unicellular life, multicellular life, our bodies and organ systems, organization of the human population on earth and what we invent and use to help us in our lives and studying the planet, the galaxies and the universe. This is further explored in the book.

BASIC UNIT

OF

LIFE

IS

THE

CELL.

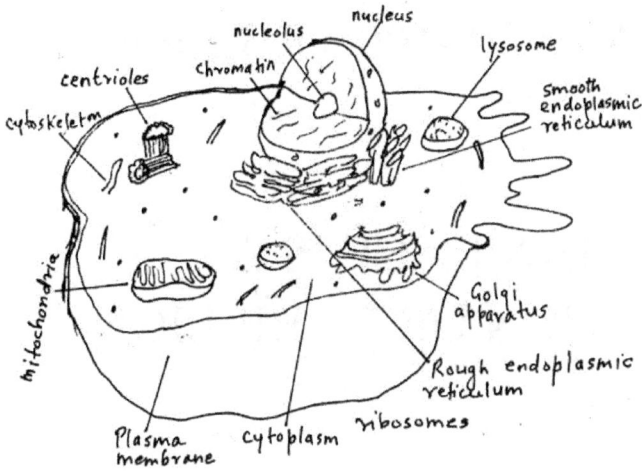

THE CELL

BASIC UNIT OF LIFE IS THE CELL.

EACH HUMAN BEING IS A
COLLECTION OF CELLS.
(ESTIMATE 30 -100 TRILLION
CELLS)

THE HUMAN RACE IS A
COLLECTION OF 7.5 BILLION
HUMANS

THE HUMAN RACE IS A
COLLECTION OF CELLS –AND
LIFE.

The CELL is the basic unit of life. Apart from this essential fact it is relevant because we are made up of approximately 30 to 100 trillion (basic units) cells.

I see the Human Being as 'one unit' with a body and a soul/consciousness. One significant feature of life and living is defined by our emotions and feelings of love, hate, pain and pleasure, sorrow and joy. This does not take away from the fact that we are essentially trillions of cells held together by connective tissue and encased by a wall/barrier of dermal-epidermal tissue called skin. We know that we are made of chemicals and elements, especially carbon and hydrogen.

It is worth studying the cell in a little more detail.

The components of the cell are –

 -cell membrane,

-Endoplasmic reticulum (smooth and rough),

- vacuole,

-nucleus,

-DNA (deoxyribonucleic acid),

- ribosome,

-Golgi,

- lysosome,

-mitochondria,

-cytoplasm.

These are made of proteins, carbohydrates, nucleic acids and fats. 90% of the weight of cell is water.

Secretions are released from the cell by exocytosis.

-The nucleus is the command center of the cell.

-The nucleolus – ribosomes are produced here.

-The Cell has chromatin which is a complex of proteins, DNA and RNA (ribonucleic acid).

-The nuclear envelope is a double membrane between nucleus and cytoplasm.

-Nuclear pore is an opening embedded with proteins that regulate passage into and out of the nucleus.

-Ribosomes are small complexes of RNA and protein which are the sites of protein synthesis.

-Peroxisome is a vesicle that contains enzymes and detoxifying potential of harmful molecules.

-Plasma membrane is a lipid bilayer in which proteins are embedded.

-Smooth endoplasmic reticulum are membranes that aid in manufacture of carbohydrates and lipids.

-Rough endoplasmic reticulum is an internal membrane studded with ribosomes that carry out protein synthesis.

-Cytoskeleton supports organelles and cell shape and plays a role in cell motion.

-Microtubule is a tube of protein molecules present in cytoplasm, centrioles, cilia and flagella.

-Intermediate filaments are intertwined protein fibers that provide support and strength.

-Actin filament are twisted protein fibers that are responsible for cell movement.

-Centriole is a complex assembly of microtubules that occurs in pairs.

-Cytoplasm is a semifluid matrix that contains the nucleus and organelles.

-Mitochondria is where energy is extracted from food during oxidative metabolism.

-Secretory vesicle is a vesicle fusing with the plasma membrane, releasing materials to be secreted from the cell.

Summary of cell functions:

-Passage and control of substances.
-Protein, carbohydrate and lipid synthesis.
-Detoxifying harmful molecules.
-Cell motion.
-Cell division.
-Protection and motion – cytoskeleton.
-Communication.
-Energy extraction from food.
-Waste – secreted out.

When life went from single cell to multicellularity approximately 50 trillion cells formed the Human Being. Cells had become specialized and formed separate organs, but they also continued to have the single cell functions.

The *human being MCO unit* has functions that mimic what the *single cell* does:

-It allows selective passage and control of substances into the body.

-It has the ability for protein, carbohydrate and lipid synthesis.

-It detoxifies harmful molecules.

-It can move/has a skeleton.

-Procreation –which involves cell division/mitosis and meiosis and is organized into producing a 'live' MCO unit 'learnt' over billions of years.

-Communication.

-Energy extraction from food.

-Waste disposal.

And, possibly, something we think makes us very different in the human being is - Emotions (which may not be entirely true as we discuss later).

So, the basic unit of life, the cell, provides the model for the multicellular unit, the Human Being, to exist – 'in its image'.

In the multicellular organism individual cells continue with their functions and also develop levels of specialization which have evolved into separate but integrated organ systems. (Neural, kidney/renal, gastrointestinal, cardiovascular/circulatory system and other systems).

The cells, 640 million years ago, formed colonies which interacted to successful multicellularity. The multicellular organism (MCO) -the human, then did the same - 'it' organized to form interactive and interdependent colonies, homes, cities and countries. The formula that life followed is what we follow - an inherent code that made the human make homes and cities that look like what the cells formed.

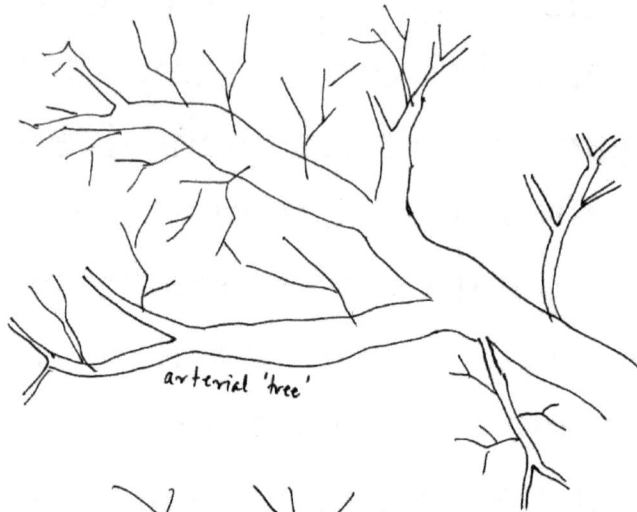

arterial 'tree'

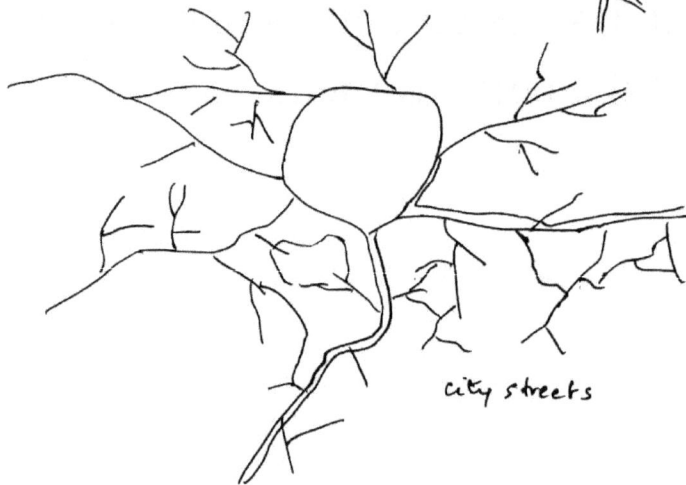

city streets

83

Our road systems which carry traffic which in turn carry people and goods of all varieties are equated commonly with the arterial and venous system which also involve traffic in the form of cells and 'goods' and distribution of nutrients/foods.

-Respiratory System: Lungs are the organs facilitating oxygen-carbon dioxide exchange. (The Humans designed the city by making something like Central Park in New York – that represent the lungs of the city. Trees produce oxygen during the day and carbon dioxide at night.).

-Gastrointestinal system: Ingestion, absorption, waste disposal, detoxifying harmful chemicals, breakdown of blood, secretion of bile, production of blood clotting mechanisms etc. The cell does this, the human body does it and the city which the human creates has similar functions where food is brought in, it is distributed, consumed, waste is collected and detoxified.

-Immune system: This provides protection against 'invading' bacteria and viruses, reaction to foreign bodies and to its own cells within the body causing autoimmune problems. The humans have specialized warrior(s) 'cells' that fight against all enemies foreign and domestic and which make up the Armed services and law enforcement agencies. These fight invading armies and from within bad actors/criminals – (autoimmune like reaction) and involves the Hematopoietic/lymphatic system.

Nervous system: This system controls voluntary and involuntary activity and emotions. I think 35 trillion cells minus 170 billion cells of the nervous system are not given enough credit for feedback to the nervous system.

In countries, cities, corporations, defense services we have developed a method of command and control in which, recently, technology and the computer has taken a major role, and which acts like a nerve center. Reliance on computers is increasing.

We Human Beings have evolved into a complex integrated 'machine' with intelligence while machines are being developed with Artificial intelligence. We can process vast amounts of information, have a larger memory (storage capacity) and reboot ourselves after sleep and rest. We made computers which were designed to process large bits of information, have a large storage capacity and boot and reboot itself when it is put into 'sleep' mode - turned on and off. Humans are developing artificial intelligence based on our existing intelligence 'system'. It looks as if man has made the computer in 'his image' - so far, without emotions. A few people can get together and form a think tank, define policy and give commands which essentially becomes a nerve center like the voluntary part of brain function.

-The reproductive system: cells divide and increase in numbers. (We 'multiply'/procreate and so increase in numbers).

-Renal and Urinary system: waste products eliminated which cells and humans and cities (organized collection of humans) do.

Skeletal system: This helps with movement of cells and humans away from danger and towards food, shelter and security. The rib cage adds additional protection for vital organs like heart and lungs and the skull provides additional protection for the Brain.

Integumentary system: provides a Border for protection – like the wall of a fort or a 'Border wall' of a country.

EMOTIONS

The world of emotions is considered to be uniquely human (though this may be an erroneous way of thinking). It is probably relevant, at this time, to try and analyze what emotions are. We can use the words we know that express what we experience when we are emotional.

Words we use are – Happiness, sadness, Fear, Anger, Surprise, Joy, Disgust, Shame, Guilt, Love, Irritation, hate, Curiosity, Greed, Depression. Amplification of happiness could be Ecstasy, sadness could intensify into grief, fear into terror and anger to rage.

The Hindi language describes some of the important emotions – feelings such as Kaam or lust, krodh or rage, lobh or greed, moh or attachment, mada or pride, matsory or jealousy. Simplification or 'deconstruction' of these myriad descriptions of emotions could be put into broad, basic, categories such as – Pleasure/pain, Positive/negative or Pleasant/unpleasant.

If we consider the simple, broad category of emotions as pleasant or unpleasant we can move away from the concept of these belonging in the central nervous system and consider them as a response of noxious or irritating stimuli and could relate it to the single non-specialized cell. Examples of these stimuli could be infection, toxins, trauma, dehydration, temperature change. A Paramecium, a single cell organism, actively moves away from a concentrated salt solution, probably, because it is 'unpleasant' and also dangerous to its well-being. We could learn from this in that we should remove ourselves from a noxious emotional environment or 'walk away' so it would not have a negative effect on our well-being.

A pleasant situation for a cell would probably mean adequate food and fluid at a suitable temperature which would mean good circulation, oxygenation, waste disposal etc.

When human beings have adequate food, shelter, clothing and no obvious threats to self and family – life would probably be considered pleasant, happy and joyful. Logically the reverse of that would be unpleasant causing apprehension, fear, unhappiness and other negative feelings/ emotions.

MULTICELLULARITY

 Single cells have been on our planet for 3.6 billion years and though there have been many 'attempts' at multicellularity – definitive multicellular life developed about 640 million years ago and has persisted till today. All single cell life did not become multicellular, so single cells continue to exist. There are 10-14 million species of multicellular organisms. We Humans have decided that we are so far, the most evolved of the species.

There are some theories about the development of multicellular organisms. Some of these are – The Symbiotic theory, The Cellularization theory, The Colonial theory, The Synzoospore theory and the role of viruses.

To address the mystery of multicellularity researchers have identified single cells available at the time and are studying them to see if the behavior of these cells can shed some light on the change to multicellularity. This is not easy as the changes occurred 640 million years ago.

It may be reasonable to start with the concept that single cells 'got together' and developed multicellular beings like Human Beings do when they formed tribes, villages, cities and countries. Trillions of cells over billions of years 'getting together' and communicating, ultimately formed a system of protected (against the elements) multicellularity with specialized organ systems.

An important question is why life needed to have the cell wall/membrane to make the viable unit of life -was it protection against the elements or against desiccation. Did the sun, the water and the winds form at the same time as life. There is supposed to be evidence that water was there before life happened.

Single cells have the ability to move and collection of cells in their multicellular forms have also developed the ability to move.

Multicellular organisms (MCO) provided the means and ability to move larger distances to find suitable environmental conditions to survive and thrive AND single cells got transported and transplanted via waste from the (GI) tract. {The human GI tract has its own cellular universe – an average of 39 trillion bacteria, nearly the same as all the cells in a human body}.

The human being was not just a mobile structure of 38 trillion cells with 39 trillion in the GI tract, but he/she was actively combating the climatic elements by finding and building structures – finding caves and then moving on to build structures like houses. A significant 'power' in the MCO's was the ability to procreate and carry a child formed by the process of meiosis over a period of nine months. So, 2 cells united to form 37 trillion cells. Interestingly, when fertilization has occurred the process continues till the baby is formed fully and then delivered to be a functioning human being.

Cells (basic units of life) form the multicellular organism (MCO's) who then get together and get organized. This 'organization' is one of life's characteristics. The MCO follows the 'Formula' and begin to get together to form villages, cities, countries and continue propagation by male and female getting together to procreate and preserve life and sustain and increase the MCO population.

Time is a unit of Deterioration

Time stops at the moment of Creation
— for that instant.

The study of the onset of multicellular life is based on the study of cells and bacteria at the time of the initiation of the multicellular form of life 1.5 billion years ago. This process has its limitations and requires scientific expertise. I suggest we can understand the process to multicellularity by studying and observing what we humans do – as in the development of civilization and cities.

Cells got together to become multicellular with the process of sticking together and developing specialized functions and through mitosis and/or meiosis. So, trillions of cells were encased in a skin and functioned as ONE unit and so the

Human Being appeared on the map of life, and this planet, 300,000 years ago. Humans wandered the face of the earth learning how to survive the elements (clothes and shelter), forage and hunt (instruments and tools), and procreate to increase absolute numbers. After 290,000 years of existence Humans decided to make life more efficient (Organize) and established the first civilization about 11,000 years ago, when the total population was 1-4 million.

Humans (People) probably came in ones and twos to gather into hundreds and thousands usually near or along a water source, which is/was a vital component for life to flourish. This is very similar to the concept of cells getting together near and in a water source to organize and function as a multicellular organism.

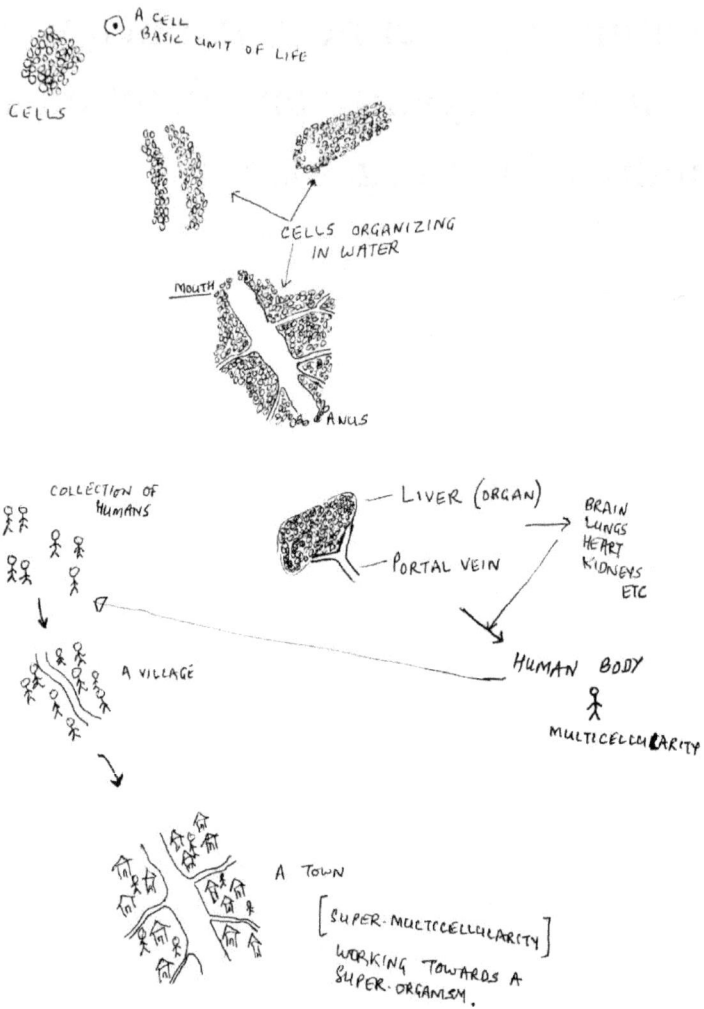

CELLS

⊙ A CELL
BASIC UNIT OF LIFE

CELLS ORGANIZING
IN WATER

MOUTH

ANUS

COLLECTION OF
HUMANS

LIVER (ORGAN)

PORTAL VEIN

BRAIN
LUNGS
HEART
KIDNEYS
ETC

A VILLAGE

HUMAN BODY

MULTICELLULARITY

A TOWN

[SUPER-MULTICELLULARITY]
WORKING TOWARDS A
SUPER-ORGANISM.

THE HUMAN BEING

The Human Being considered here to represent life did the next 'natural' thing – build a wall around itself in the form of a hut/house which is what organelles did to become the basic unit of life – build a wall. These Humans who had got together and built little houses (with walls) then collectively built another wall around the 'city' to fortify itself. {Built a Fort – a practice by humans for centuries}. These house walls, fort walls always had doors and windows, the doors being used for exit and ingress of goods, materials and fellow humans. This is similar to cell membranes/cell walls which allow ingress and egress of nutrition and waste and other materials through 'doors'/ receptors. Entry and exit in a human's house is allowed after a knock on the door or ringing a doorbell. The guest is identified and allowed in which is what a cell probably does through its membrane or wall. It identifies friend and foe and allows entry.

House walls, Fort walls are breached by enemies, foes and invaders who use force or deceit on the wall or the doors. This may be similar to injury and death of cells that have damage inflicted by invaders, toxins, irritants viruses etc.

As people collected in groups, they organized. They had to communicate to establish governance and to establish hierarchy (which seems to be an important aspect of human existence) and specialization. Each person in this new community would be asked to declare or explore their skills which would help the community, for example – hunters, warriors, builders, administrators, healers/physicians, waste disposal specialists - and out of these would emerge leaders. This could indicate that within us there exist leader cells/organs and a possible hierarchical system.

Civilization, around the water source, a river, then formed on both sides of the waterway. Not only was water an absolute essential for life to flourish but it was also used as a path for distribution of materials for daily living, using boats and water 'traffic'. Before the concept of careful, sanitized waste disposal was developed waste was just dumped into the water to be carried away from the inhabited area.

This human experience is similar to the theory of how multicellular life formed with single cells around a water source. Channels (canals) carrying water were developed and taken from the main river to serve areas of habitation away from the original water source and making it more connected and become organized to make an 'organism'. These water channels are similar, in the human being, to the vascular system to the point of calling roads in towns and freeways as the arterial system. Roads have been divided into a system that carries traffic both ways, again, similar to the vascular system where blood is carried away from the heart by arteries and to the heart by veins. We have traffic lights that regulate traffic, but the human body does not have traffic lights and has a smooth flow (literally) of blood. Does this mean that we should design our traffic system to flow with merging and diverging roads everywhere, so traffic never stops? To further analyze this, do traffic lights help mimic the pulsatile phenomenon that our arterial system has.

On the way to multicellularity, cells formed a tube around their water source in a way in which food enters the 'mouth' and waste left on the other end which is called the cloaca, which, in the human later, became the anus.

Cities then grew in size and complexity. There were Kingdoms, States and Countries but the formula of the organization has remained the same and is reproducible around the world. Similar habitations were established, in different time zones, by humans at a time when communication and exchange of ideas was not easy or even possible.

 The Human Being has not had any significant anatomical change in the last 300,000 years. Organs like liver, brain, spleen, kidney, lungs, with their specialized cells stay in their place and carry out their functions with a constant supply of essentials carried by the blood.

This may indicate that Humans will organize into localized concentration of occupied housing units where people would not have to leave home because all necessary goods for survival would be provided along with virtual entertainment of every sort.

Entertainment appears to be extremely important to the Human Being.

This is already happening in the development of the concept of self-sustaining habitat, so people do not need to travel much for work, and we would function like an efficient body organ. The Neuro-vascular system carries, provides and interprets all the information that is required by the 'cell colonies'/organs. Do Human Beings, who love music and entertainment, which includes participating in sports – playing, competing and watching, have an equivalent activity for cells and organ systems? {What is the equivalent of 'having fun' at the cellular level?} This is a very significant part of human existence.

Music is supposed to release dopamine in the brain and cause a pleasurable feeling.

Sports, instead of war, can help us strategize and compete without killing and have entertainment value.

The question is whether the brain represents the rest of the cells in the body when exposed to a pleasant experience and 'speaks' for them (trillions) or somehow the pleasant/pleasurable sensations are transmitted to all cells and if that is the case how does it happen so quickly? Does this happen through the blood, nerves or both? If it is with vibration, which is what music is, then maybe the sound effects the brain and the vibration can reach all the cells. This would explain the centuries old accepted chanting of Ohm to bring peace to the whole body and mind during meditation and prayer. When the body and mind is agitated or anxious, I have tried to chant

Ohm or have a friendly conversation and it seems to have a calming influence. I have often wondered why 'crazy' people talk to themselves. Does the vibration of the voice make them, and their cells feel calmer - reinforcing that somebody is still in command? It is important for the brain to feel good and so make the body feel good also. (And vice-versa?).

Another example to see the importance of making the non-neuro cells feeling good is during orgasm. The sensation throughout the whole body may be important as information in the form of this signal to all body cells that a significant event as occurred and may prepare the body for conception.

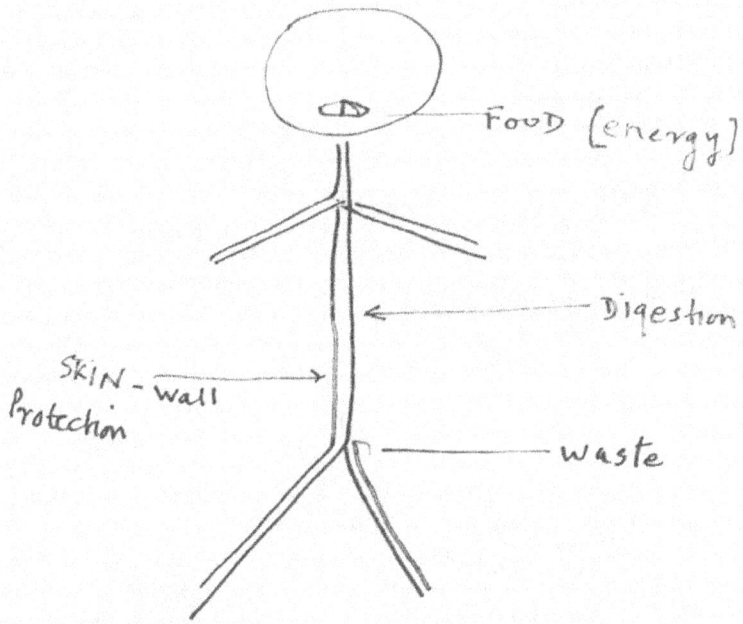

FOOD (energy)

Digestion

SKIN – wall
Protection

waste

HUMAN
30-40 trillion cells.

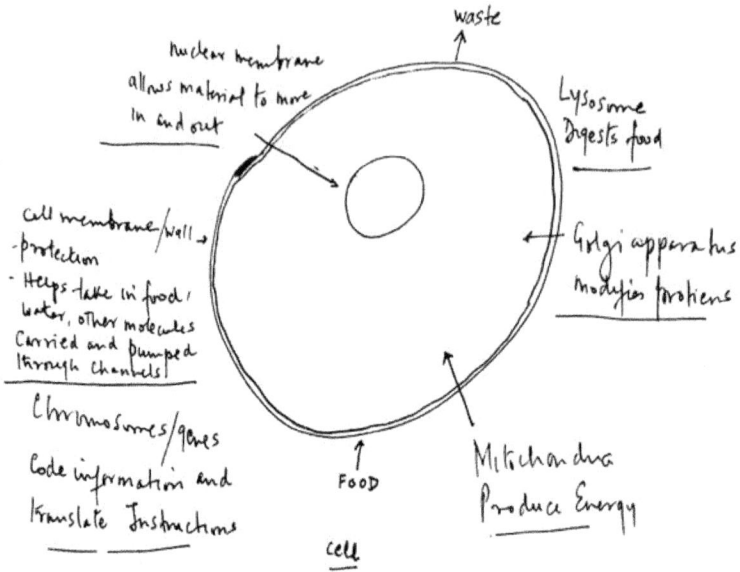

nuclear membrane
allows material to move
in and out

Cell membrane/wall
- protection
- Helps take in food,
water, other molecules
Carried and pumped
through channels

Chromosomes/genes
Code information and
translate Instructions

waste

Lysosome
Digests food

Golgi apparatus
modifies proteins

FOOD

Mitochondria
Produce Energy

cell

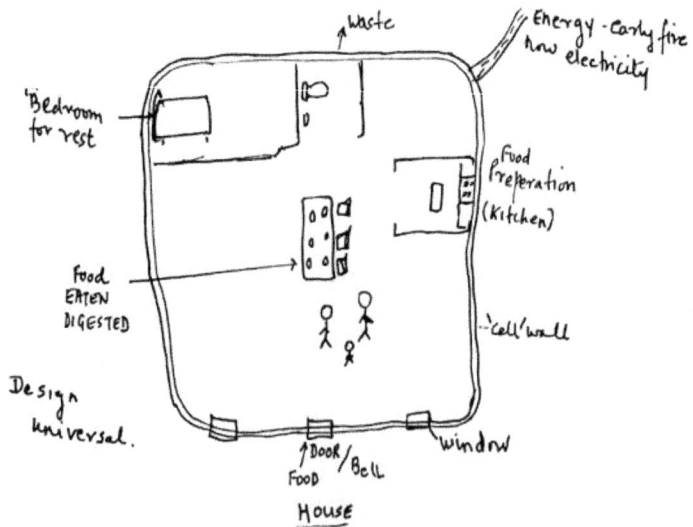

Bedroom
for rest

Food
Preparation
(Kitchen)

Food
EATEN
DIGESTED

Design
universal.

waste

Energy - Early fire
now electricity

'cell' wall

window

DOOR/Bell
FOOD

HOUSE

Will the human race become the human organism modeled after the Human Being, which was a few billion years in the making?

The relatively recent development of computers and the Internet has been an important part of the connectivity of the Human species. It is noteworthy that in common parlance the neurological system is likened to the brain which controls the nerves that supply all organ systems. The human, as a 'computer', has been around for 300,000 years. Life has the ability to gather information, analyze it, store it and reproduce it and also provides answers to problems.

All the systems in the body are dependent on electrical impulses and it

is not much of a surprise - though a
great achievement-

Brain	Computer
Database	Database
memory	Memory
Analysis	Analysis (Programs)
Solutions	Solutions
Sleep/awake	Switch off / Re-boot
Controls certain organs	Can control 'machines' eg fly the plane.
Intelligence	'Artificial' intelligence

[input, storage, processing, output]

that humans could produce, harness
and use electricity.

Similarity of the human body's organized internal response is similar to the external 'human unit' response as seen in the basic injury/damage response. (The pothole example) – the road gets an 'injury' and develops a pot hole which could be dangerous to passing humans, so, it needs to be repaired. Once the damage is identified a call is made to the appropriate department and skilled workers (specialized cells) are sent to clean it up, put in repair material, cover the surface and make it safe and functional again. When a body is injured signals are sent which get a response by specialized cells being sent to the site of injury where cleaning / debriding is carried out followed by repair and restoration to as normal as possible.

The Universe

We live on planet Earth which, incidentally, has an orbital speed of 67,000 miles per hour and rotational speed at the equator of 1000 miles per hour, and we exist as part of The Universe. It is worth taking a look at our cell-estial environment.

My address for anyone out there in the Universe is –

California, USA, Planet Earth, The Solar system, The Milky way, The Universe. P.O. Box can be added.

It might take a while for a package to get to me from the outer reaches of the Universe as there are 120-300 sextillion (10 to the power of 23) stars in the observable Universe, which spans 93 billion light years. A light year is the distance light travels in one year (approximately 6 trillion miles and a trillion is 10 to the power of 12). The Humans' intellectual capacity makes some kind of sense of these astronomical numbers – no pun intended. Our extremely small and insignificant size, relative to these numbers, is only made relevant by the size of our ego, imagination and ambition. (We can travel to the moon and plan on colonizing mars.)

This may also provide an indication of our metastatic character and the need to spread. This would also lend credence to the Seeding theory of life on this planet.

As we stand on the surface of our planet and look into space we wonder about the distances and how enormous they are and our role in the Universe and how we got here. All those Humans who believe in the Creator and look to the heavens and pray must then believe that there is life in the form of the Creator who is linked to us with Divine threads of existence and communication.

I can imagine putting myself in the place of a single cell in the human body and gazing up and around and seeing a vast Universe in which I exist - one cell amidst maybe 50 trillion cells. It is not difficult to imagine this cell and all cells feel connected to this life force and to feel to be in the presence of a Creator. The Universe has been divided into regular matter (4%), Dark matter (23%) and Dark Energy (73%). There is not much known about Dark matter and Dark energy. The 73% is an interesting number as it relates so closely to the 75% which is the amount of water in the Human infant and which comes down to 50 – 65% in the adult. 73% of the Earth's surface is covered with water.

Is Dark energy of the Universe the same as our water on the planet and water in the body. Planet Earth has 73% water and if we relate this number to the

Human then as life on the planet continues, into adulthood, will our water level drop to the 50 -65 %, in a thousand, million or a billion years. Another similar coincidence is the 100 trillion atoms in a cell and up to 100 trillion cells in the Human Body though there is a wide range estimate of the number of cells in the human (10 to 100 trillion). There are about 10 trillion planets in our galaxy and 10 to the power of 24 planets in the Universe. The most widely accepted theory of the birth of the Universe is the Big bang. (13.8 billion years ago). This theory does not shed any light on what it was that 'exploded' and expanded into what our Universe is as we know it. This then certainly gives us the freedom to imagine what could have occurred at that particular instant of the formation of the Universe with the Big Bang. It could have been a collision of a very fast projectile into a celestial body containing nuclear elements, which all stars have, creating an explosion that resulted in the formation of our universe. Cooling then occurred and radiation levels decreased (half-life of uranium is 4.5 billion years) and conditions became compatible for life to 'happen' as per previously mentioned theories or we were already on a planet with immense density and were 'destroyed' by a blast of radiation like in the treatment of cancer.

It took 9.2 billion years for Earth to form and another 1.4 billion years for life to show itself.

We have trillions of stars and planets in galaxies which make up the Universe. If each multicellular organism, on our planet, is imagined as a universe or galaxy (having billions/ trillions of cells) then all the plants, trees, animals and insects are the models of the single Universe or multiple Universes of varying shapes and sizes. There are areas on Earth, like the Sahara Desert, where nearly nothing grows, which would represent the lacunae of space where there is nothing but 'space'.

We exist. This fact can start us on a path of scientific and thoughtful exploration – like addressing the age-old question of why we exist (difficult to say), how we came to be and where are we 'going' from here?

THE FORMULA

A major revelation in my study of life, cells and humans is that life's' secrets and methods are revealed by our behavior as humans and how we behave gives us a glimpse of life's formula. The previous pages in this book have built a base of 'cellular thought' and how life may have started and how life's manifestation has emerged. This has probably followed the direction that the immense amount of information in its code has provided and, according to our time scale and standards, it has taken a very, very long time to come to this point of our existence.

The theory that I will 'cell' you is based on how humans (as representatives of other multicellular organisms) do things – to organize, grow, reproduce, respond to external stimuli and maintain ourselves (homeostasis) as Life does, at the cellular level and in our bodies.
The most basic element in the formation of life is the collection of organelles with the development of the cell wall/membrane around them. This is similar to what we do as humans. We have our own 'wall' called the skin that contains and protects trillions of cells that make up the human body. We humans find it extremely important to make and live in a house/hut that is essentially a wall around us. This is our

'cell wall'. Our 'homeless' do not have their 'cell walls' and are a very vulnerable section of humanity. They are a source of emotional discontent to those of us who have homes and most people feel the need to provide the homeless with a home. {A protective wall, An essential need}.

A family will build a home, and a collection of families will build a collection of homes and put a wall around them making a Fort/Castle. These are also protective and functional. Like cells, which have receptors and the ability to allow or not to allow substances to enter or leave, houses/forts/castles have doors, windows, sentries, door bells, which

also allows selective entry and exit,
behave like the cellular receptors.
Is the cell more safe and secure with its
mechanisms or are we more secure with
our techniques? Can we learn from
the cell and can we apply to the cell
what we do, for example drug delivery?
We build computers which have
security barriers called firewalls for
additional protection against
unauthorized access. This is what a cell
does, a body does and what we as a
collection of humans do. In a state of
good health, the normal cell will allow
substances to enter that have the correct
'asking code' and those that interrogate
the cell appropriately will enter and

carry out the functions they are supposed to.

Extrapolation from this concept/formula shows that it is natural for a country to have borders (wall) that protects against illegal entry/migration and require visas to legally enter when verifiable information has been provided to the authorities. A cell wall provides entry to substances probably for a specific function so it makes sense to only allow individuals to come into a country who can contribute to the wellness and success of that country. Even tourists contribute to the economy. Does a body have 'tourist cells' – visiting cells from different organs?

The cell wall is extremely important. The earth, with life on it, has developed an 'atmospheric cell wall' and become like a cell. Life 'organelles' on earth would not survive without this cell wall which takes us back to the basic unit of life being the cell with a wall. Extrapolation of this idea is that however large the Universe is, it is probably 'contained' by some kind of a cell wall – the skin of the Universe. The integrity or health of a cell can be compromised by adverse conditions like starvation and toxic stimuli and can recover if these conditions are reversed in time. Similarly, defense of a community within a Fort can be compromised by a siege from an invading army, leading to starvation of those within who become weak and vulnerable to physical assault by the 'invader' with the defense being overcome resulting in its ultimate surrender ending in its death or subjugation.

When a body is 'fighting' an infection the defending cells of the body can defeat the invading bacteria and win and recover or succumb to the assault and die in great numbers (pus). This could be localized to a small area or this infection/ invasion can spread and kill the body. {The intriguing part is that 'guest' and 'host' both die so the purpose is not clear of this entire process!}. If the person survives it gets 'stronger' developing immunity for the next assault. The similarity with this process is that if the invading army is beaten back strategies are developed for a better defense/offence. In war many people die and must be 'removed' from the field – the 'pus' of war. Inflammation results due to an irritant reacting with the immune system of the body. The irritant can win, or the body can win. The person can recover, develop a chronic illness or die. This immunity is an extremely vital function of the human body. In USA 300 million functioning units (humans) in the country have organized to respond to an irritant – foreign (non-self) or domestic (self). The 'stronger' the antigen, the 'stronger' the antibody response but would depend on the health of the individual where immunity was not compromised for example by a foreign power sowing seeds of division and chaos for years.

The phenomenon of the acute, excessive, unexplained inflammatory response of some people in the USA to Donald Trump (domestic antigen) has been worthy of study. This significant inflammatory response can be injurious to the country if not resolved. Resolution can occur with removal of the antigen by the strong immune reaction or by the army of 'self' becoming active and overcoming the other antibodies. If neither occurs, it become a constant state of division which will ultimately weaken the country/ host. The other way of resolution is by the antigen forming its own antibodies like a vaccine to protect the organism/country against a strong inflammatory response.

It would appear, from studying the attack on a castle, that the vulnerable points would be the gates and windows, and this might be like vulnerable points of a cell wall which could be used to destroy the cell or save it.
Our houses, castles, borders have always been under assault by other humans. Does this mean that a significant reason for our ill health is

related to attacks of cells vs cells or like vs like indicating a predominance of autoimmune problems?

Is color of the skin (race) an aggravating factor for conflict and will this disappear in the future to bring peace and make it a harmonious organism?

Local battles amongst humans may be like local inflammation in the body. A bigger systemic upheaval in the body may be like an international crisis – like a world war, which may take longer to resolve. Totalitarian regimes in the second world war were defeated by Democratic alliances (except Russia). It is unknown how different the world would have been had the 'other' side won. The human race would have carried on with a different 'culture'. The human race has not obliterated itself yet, but, it is possible that it can. Species do get extinct quite commonly. If that did happen, life, in other forms, would still carry on. New species are being discovered regularly.

Time, as we know it, seems to be on the side of the tough, resilient single cell forms which have survived for billions of years. Are multicellular life forms as resilient?

The cell, a single unit, collected 30 to 50 trillion cells around it to form a bigger single unit – one human being. Now, are 7.5 billion human 'units' organizing into a single super unit – a functioning Human Organism.

Will this 'super' organism organize to send parts of itself to other parts of the Universe (like metastatic cancer). This provides a basis of analyzing the link between life, the planet, the Universe and beyond.

If we think about the seeding theory of life and that we came across and through space, from another entity, it might explain what we consider God would or could be – like a parent, and would fit into the idea that we are God's creation and have been created in His/Her image.

5 billion out of 7.5 billion people think there is a God. Prophets have preached,

and people have believed. Do these people have an extra something in their 'genetic' makeup of cells that makes them believe in the presence of the creator?

Does the formation of cities/towns, with the gathering of people at one place indicate how single cells get together to form multicellular functioning organisms?

Does the MCO, a Human Being, function in a manner that indicates how a city/town/country functions and vice versa?

Does the study of how Humans plan our cities and how they function indicate how we could do better in looking after or treating our bodies?

When a patient comes into my medical office usually the first thing done is the measurement of the vital signs (Blood pressure, heart rate, respiratory rate, temperature) and height and weight. Normal values have been established and any abnormal value indicates deviation from a state of being healthy. Every organization, corporation, city, state and country should have a set of 'vital signs' that can be monitored to show the state of 'health'. {Birth and death rate, population (number and density), level of education, unemployment, access to health care etc.}.

The health of the planet should be monitored by things like level of pollution, disease etc.

These indices should be maintained within a narrow spectrum of normality. Baseline measurements should be taken and then can be monitored for change. Raised temperature of a body is a sign of illness. (A superheated economy in a country?)

Raised blood pressure (increased tension in the blood vessel) is a potentially lethal problem within a human. In a conflict between two groups of humans we often talk about 'tensions boiling over'. Raised temperature, tensions, blood pressure must all be 'treated' to bring conditions to normality.

When trillions of cells got together it was important to regulate the conditions for optimal function (homeostasis). This included regulation of Ph (acidity and alkalinity), pO_2 and CO_2 (oxygen and carbon dioxide), sodium, calcium and glucose. Example - if blood pressure rises the stretch receptors in the aorta and carotid sinus are stimulated. This information is sent via nerves to the medulla oblongata (Brain stem). Motor nerves take the message back to the heart and small arterioles which dilate and brings the blood pressure to normal. Homeostasis would be a good system to have built for cities where thousands/millions of humans live and work together, so normality could be attained at the start of any negative occurrence.

The obvious success of the cell is that it has continued life for billions of years, yet cell death is a normal process. Cell division and reproduction is obviously greater than the death rate for life to continue. So, a declining birth rate of a population could not be a good sign. Does the Human Body function 'smoothly' because all cells are governed under strict rules possibly by one organ or a hierarchical system of ruling organs?

Could this mean that the world would function better under a global governance structure or Dictatorship? We value our freedoms and prefer Democracy as a system of government, but this probably would not work for a human body, with each cell having a vote.

If Hitler, Mussolini and the Japanese had won the second world war would the resulting 'world' be very different? The human body is maintained with a certain degree of efficiency and tight controls 'perfected' over billions of years. We emulate our body systems by examples of roads and streets in towns which we commonly refer to as arteries (the arterial system) and do our best with rules and laws to maintain a healthy flow of traffic on these 'arteries'.

Within the human being there are cells that defend, attack and protect against other cells and agents that would harm us and these cells also have a protective mechanism forming an organ like the skin (Integumentary system). The human being has organized itself into specialized 'organ systems' like the Defense Forces, the Law Enforcement agencies, the Border Patrol. (Our Immune System).

The communication system in our bodies is well established through the autonomic and somatic systems. These are Involuntary and Voluntary. A hot object touching the skin results in a reflex involuntary withdrawal away from the 'bad' stimulus. We have developed 'involuntary' actions like the fire sprinklers that turn on to put out a fire. If we see a fire, we know the danger and voluntarily we will stay away from it or at least stay a safe distance from it.

Salivation on seeing food is involuntary and it helps us prepare for eating and digestion, but we can choose to eat when we want to. (Voluntary) but, we are driven to eat when hunger overcomes us and makes us eat, to live and to survive. Thirst can be controlled only up to a point, but it will make us drink. Movement of the bowel,

peristalsis, is not under voluntary
control. Discharge of waste to a degree
is voluntary so we can choose a time
but ultimately the body will get rid of it.
All these responses are geared for
survival even though the ultimate fate is
death.
Humans have also developed
complicated and extensive systems of
communicating but early on it was
smoke signals, drums, written
messages, telephones, internet and then,
to it, was added code and encryption.
Electrical, mechanical and chemical
pathways work in the Human Body and
similar pathways are present in what the
Human Beings make.

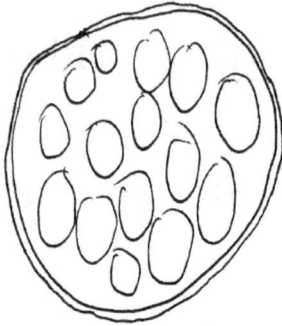

Electric Cable
Cross-section

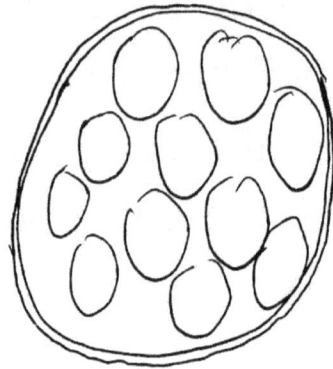

nerve
Cross-section

The cross section of a nerve shows
discrete nerve bundles and the cross
section of an electric cable shows a
similar structure enclosed in a sheath.
Other thought-provoking similarities of
what cells created to form the human
body are the lungs for oxygen and

carbon-dioxide exchange and 'green' areas in cities, a prime example being Central Park in New York - the lungs of the city.

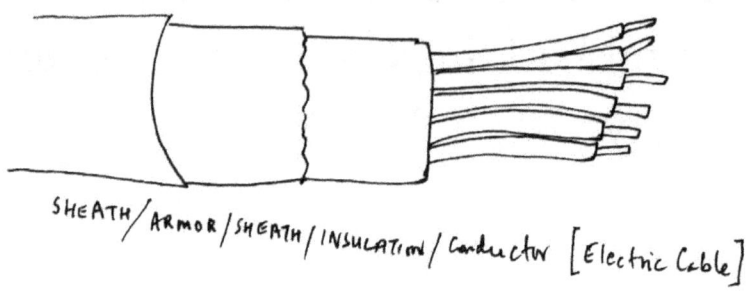

SHEATH / ARMOR / SHEATH / INSULATION / Conductor [Electric Cable]

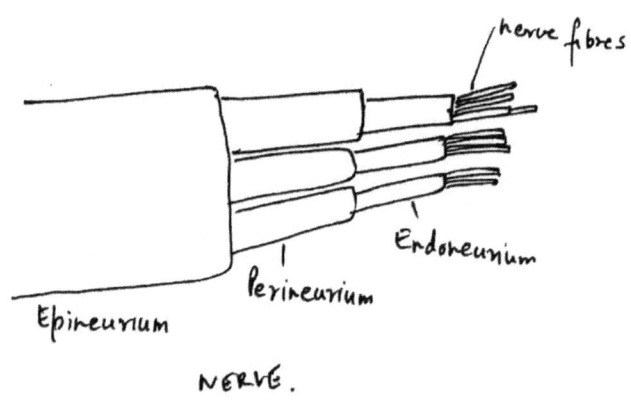

nerve fibres

Endoneurium

Perineurium

Epineurium

NERVE.

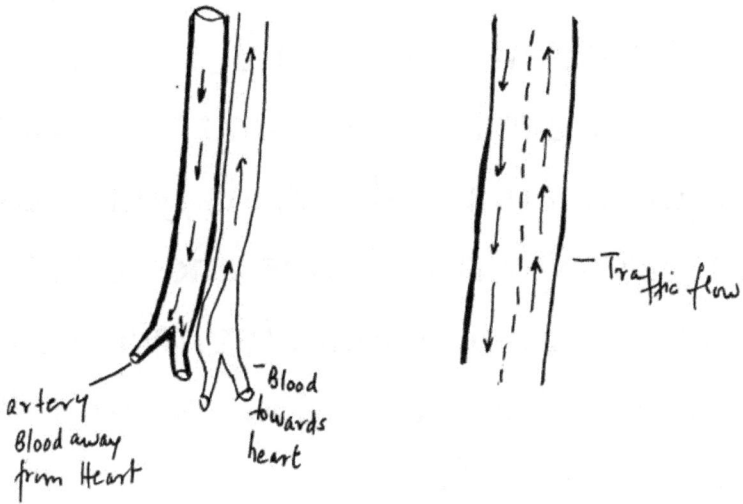

artery
Blood away
from Heart

– Blood
towards
heart

– Traffic flow

[can we learn from blood flow to help with traffic?]

In the body, cells are transported great distances in the arterial and venous systems. Humans move great distances on the roads – our 'arterial' system. These roads have the same design as does the vascular system in the body. The artery carries blood and cells away from the heart and the veins lying next to the artery carries blood and cells to the heart. The roads and highways carry traffic both ways to and away from the 'heart' of the city.

 Our transport system and mode of travel has evolved a lot over the years – walking from one point to the other, using a horse to go faster and further, inventing the wheel, the horse and carriage, the motor car, the train, the airplane, the raft, the canoe, the boat, the submarine and the mighty aircraft carrier. (Metastatic behavior).

Building in our image: The motor car engine encased in a body was built with connecting 'organ' systems, but it comes 'alive' when the human gets in and starts the engine and it can then be controlled to go where the human wants it. The human uses the vehicle to go to the office, shopping, go visiting and then brings it back to where it started. (Back to base/home).
It may be that circulating cells may be taken to specific areas by 'drivers' that control the cell and take it to where it has to go.

We live in a house. It has electricity, heating, a kitchen to make food, a bed to rest in, a toilet for waste. Cells have organelles, make proteins, maintain a certain temperature and remove waste. As a rule, houses do not move. We enter and leave a house as we like. We shut it down when we leave using keys which only work for our house. We also go to work by getting into a car. We go out to our office to work and keep the organism working. We take a ride back to home where we come, to rest. Our circulating cells are vehicles which take on passengers, drivers and go to the places where they are required to be. In the body cells are transported in fluid. Humans made roads to travel on.

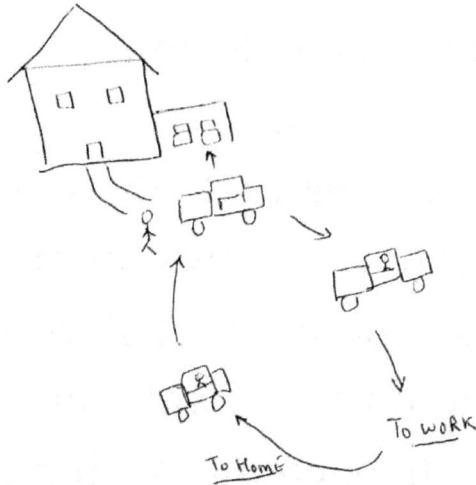

Are cells in the body 'vehicles' that take 'worker material' back and forth?

In the body the cells are carried in the bloodstream to a site where there is a collection of cells forming an organ fixed in one place.

Will we eventually do the same thing? All things required by a human – groceries, clothes etc. will be delivered to each home by 'circulating cells. This is already happening in a limited fashion. (drones etc.). There are already self-driving vehicles which can take and deliver required objects from one place to another. This is happening in a very limited fashion and will take a lot of time to be fully connected and functioning all over the planet as the human body has done (that took a few billion years).

'Man' is a gregarious animal, so humans exist in societies which exist and succeed by having a common goal of survival and living by rules and laws but catering to certain needs. An important aspect of the human is the need for pleasure but not pain. Now with the development of digital and virtual worlds humans will find less need to 'go out' to seek pleasure, entertainment and company and be happier to live together in close knit collections (human organs e.g. liver). The human body has its vital organs and they are connected by blood, vessels, nerves, and tissue. It is a system that works. The city has a similar structure with the 'heart of the city', its arterial system of roads, its people (cells), and its governance. Will the world ever come to exist by what I think, as 'the law of multicellularity' that people and continents will work as a unit.

Hierarchy. Leadership. Organizational structure.
The human body with 35 trillion cells appears to work smoothly, with all organ systems working seamlessly for the greater good or common objective of leading a healthy life. It is not clear if one organ system is at the top of the pecking order, 'telling' other organs what to do or if all organs participate in a way that the burden of successful

living is equally shared thus having a 'flat' organizational structure.

In observing the Human race, 7.5 billion people, we see that we need a command and control structure.

In the family we have a 'head' of the family. In a corporation we have a CEO. The country is led by a President or Prime Minister. In the military we have a General or a Commanding Officer and a Supervisor on a factory floor. (In a wolf pack there is a leader, a Queen bee in a hive and leaders in Gorillas, elephants and lions.) This might indicate that we have a system of 'Leadership' cells in our bodies that get the other cells to do their jobs.

Kings and Dictators have ruled millions of people over the centuries. It is interesting to consider the factors that can allow one person to rule over millions and have absolute power over so many. In these situations, power has been seized and maintained through methods fair and foul. Hierarchy and leadership are important to the Human. In a democracy a leader is elected freely and then given the power to govern or 'rule'.

People have consistently shown the desire to form empires and subjugate conquered civilizations - "Global Domination".

This may be an indication of unifying all people functioning as one unit - like cells forming a human body and all these distinct human bodies forming the Human Organism.

Domination has been attempted through religion (Christianity and Islam) or ideology (Communism). It has taken 300,000 years to come to this point of human existence and it may take a while to work out how humans will survive as a species but studying the human body may show us the way. Humans have been at war with each other since the beginning and the reason for this is not always clear. If we take the premise of the human being functioning like the human organism, we might be able to understand how the body and the cells within it function.

It appears that the ultimate goal of the Human race is to try and 'run' this world in the manner the Human Body is organized and 'run' –

This will be achieved by Global Domination, by a people using race/religion or ideology such as communism.

Or

Achieving a Global Collaborative Structure (GCS) of people/ countries developing specialties and working together to benefit the Human Organism.

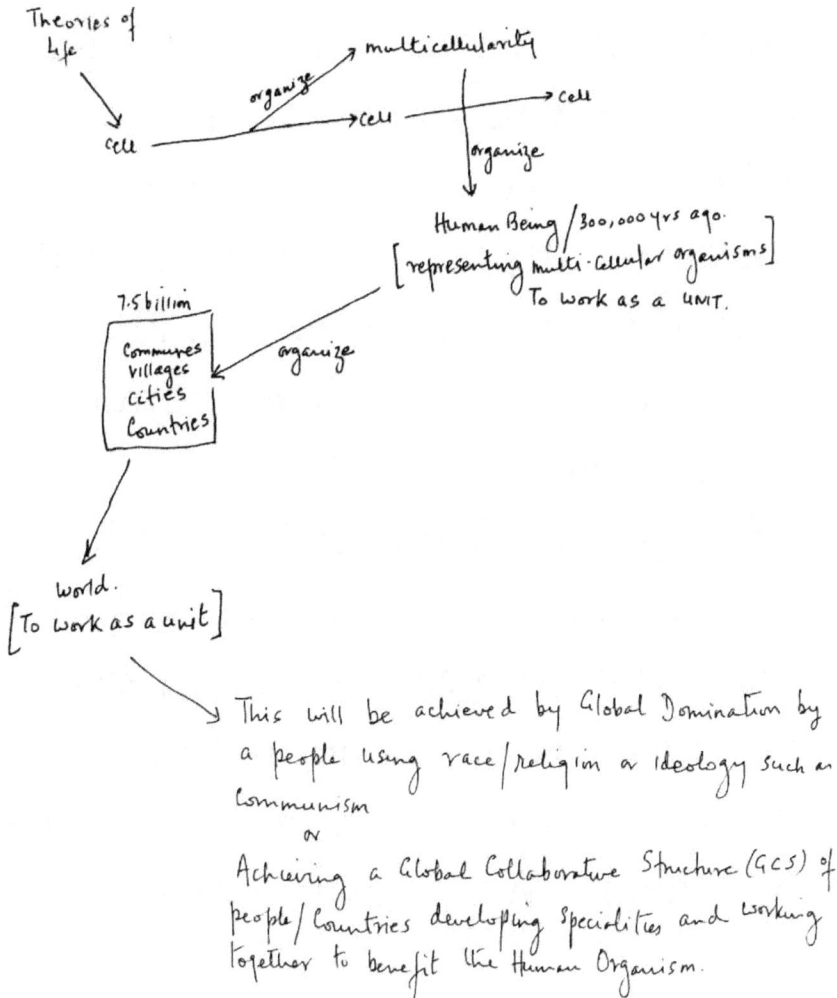

Theories of
Life

cell → cell —organize→ cell → multicellularity

multicellularity → cell

cell —organize→ Human Being / 300,000 yrs ago.
[representing multi-cellular organisms]
To work as a UNIT.

—organize→

7.5 billion
Communes
Villages
Cities
Countries

world.
[To work as a unit]

This will be achieved by Global Domination by a people using race/religion or ideology such as Communism

or

Achieving a Global Collaborative Structure (GCS) of people/Countries developing Specialties and working together to benefit the Human Organism.

166

We will ultimately do what the cell has done. What has happened in the past billions of years shows us a path to the future and evolution. If we are a metastatic deposit of malignant cells we will be destroyed, or we will kill our host - though we originate from the host, parent or God.

 If we are the first ever form of life, we should study ourselves and our past for the billions of years we have existed - it will possibly reveal our future.

Time and distance are our friends and our enemy. WE live on yet *we* die.

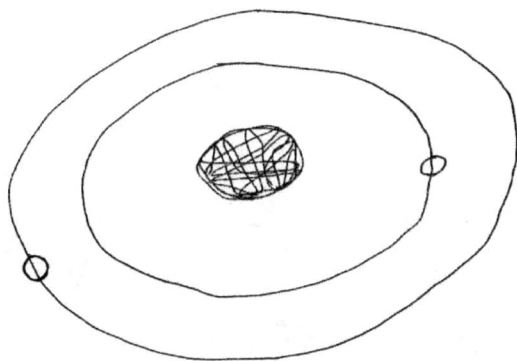

PLANETS

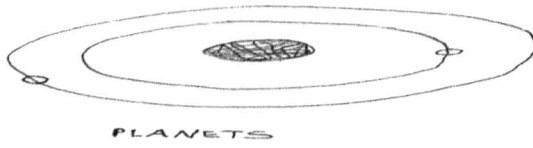

PLANETS

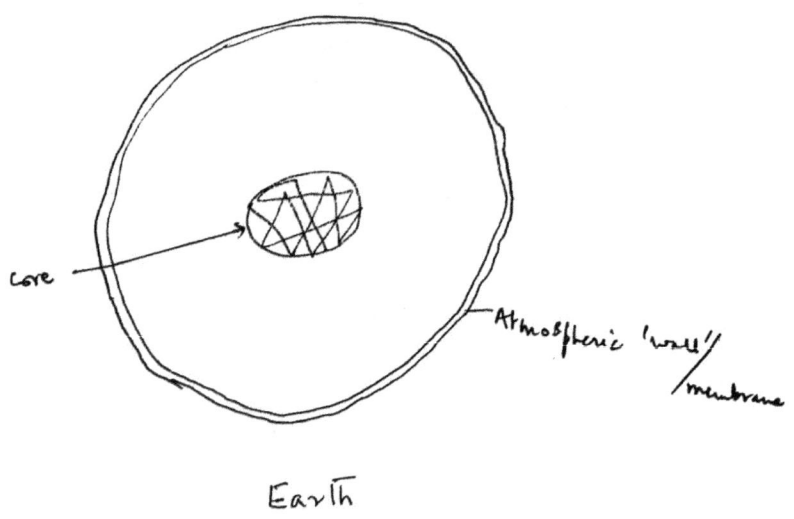

core

Atmospheric 'wall'/membrane

Earth

169

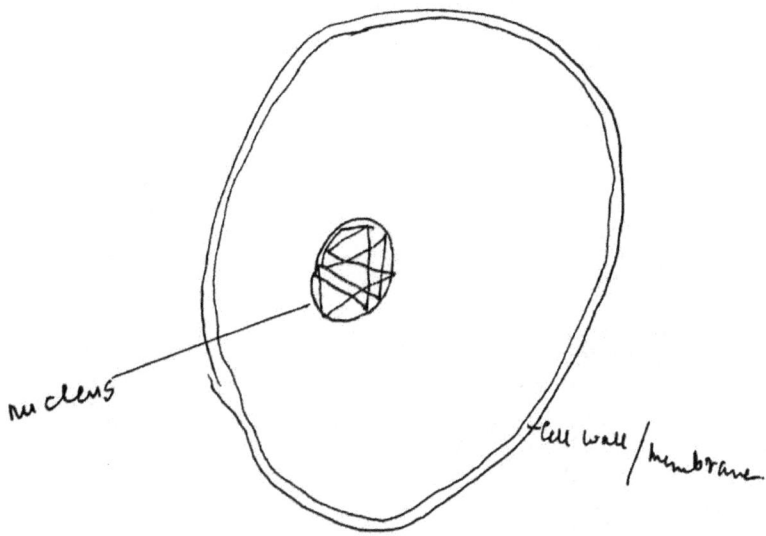

nucleus

cell wall / membrane

cell

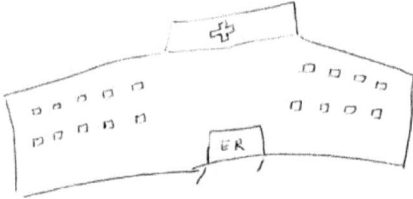

HOSPITALS / HEALTH CARE FACILITIES
FOR THE SICK AND DYING.

Humans recycle bones,
Skin and other tissues.

[also break down old or
damaged blood cells.]

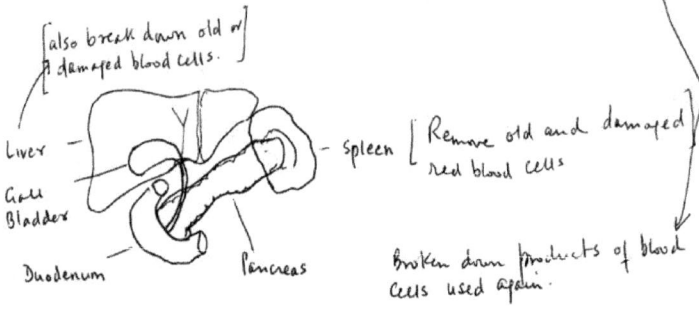

Liver —

Gall
Bladder

Duodenum   Pancreas

— spleen [Remove old and damaged
          red blood cells

Broken down products of blood
cells used again.

Is there a 'Hospital' in the body?

Human Being with
Soul.

Human Dies
Soul is released.

Living Human
Receives 'soul'
in the form of
'memories' and
dead person's legacy.

Some final thoughts.

We commonly talk about 'Body and soul'. We have talked about the body. Now, to spend a moment on the soul and atman. I have not been able to find a very satisfactory definition or explanation of these words which have been a venerated concept for centuries and believed by followers of Christianity, Islam, Judaism, Hinduism and Sikhism. The soul in my way of thinking is that when a person dies, he/she leaves only memories in the minds of people and these are stored in neural cells. So, the soul is never destroyed as it is carried by the living and may be a form of re- incarnation. The soul is carried in all people who had a significant interaction with those who have passed on.

In the medical world death is declared when brain death occurs which can occur after 5 minutes of oxygen deprivation. It is interesting that during surgery on an extremity we use a tourniquet which can prevent blood from coming into the limb for up to 90 minutes - so no perfusion, no oxygen and when tourniquet is released there is no damage to the cells of the limb.

In a person who is declared dead after 5 to 10 minutes there are 35 trillion cells which take much longer to die and are generally ignored at that moment.

Many people believe that the body is just a vessel for carrying the soul in life's journey. I find it difficult to ignore 35 trillion cells that are the basic units of life and think of 'them' as a vessel or a carrier.

Let's not forget or take for granted - the little guy/gal - the cell. Cells are everywhere, they are organized and resilient and have survived billions of years. They deserve our respect.

face

House

Car

Electric Cable
cross-section

herve
cross-section

176

Conclusion

The cell is the basic unit of life, yet it is a highly complex mechanism which over billions of years has formed the multicellular organism. In this book the human being has been taken as a representative of the MCO. The synergistic and harmonious functioning of the organ systems forming the human is truly a biological wonder. 7.5 billion humans are living, working and dying on this planet, which itself is working as a cell. These 7.5 billion humans will have to learn to live with one another to become THE MCO so it can live the synergistic and harmonious way the cell achieved the formation of the human being.

Brief points –

-P53 protein checks chromosomes and if damage is severe the cell is forced to die.

-Process of cellular death exists within the genetic code.

 -Hayflick limit is 120 years – maximum number of years a Human can live.

Some poems from

INVISIBLE HANDS
    A BOOK OF POETRY

HARKI DHILLON

Available at amazon.com

Surgery

Hands move
in controlled ecstasy,
immersed in
nature's beauty gone wrong.
The depths are exposed
illuminated by
artificial light
and the wisdom of years.
The dance of the fingers
choreographed by experience,
synchronous
with the aim
of initiating
a cure
of a malady

inflicting
this unfortunate body.

A Human Life

A brilliant flash
 of light
reflected off
a grain of sand.
A zillion stars
a trillion miles
a billion years,
the Universe.
A human life,
just a brilliant flash
reflected off
a grain of sand.

ICU

The rhythmic puffing
sounds of hope,
merged with despair,
mingle with a prayer,
interwoven
with the sighs of unanswered questions.

The curtain, apologetically,
Is half drawn,
A boundary
As definite
As a two foot
thick wall.

The fluorescent lights
And voices outside,

A stark contrast
To the silence and semi-darkness within
The room
And in my soul.

Another presence,
an encouraging smile,
deft hands
manipulate, assess
and record
the lingering, struggling,
dormant
signs of life.

This is just the
tenth day,
a lifetime, already,
yet

hope lives
because
it is the tenth day.

I wake up on
the eleventh day,
dreading the visit
but
eager to sit in my
chair, in the left
hand corner at the
foot of the bed.

I arrive,
bathed and dressed
and spruced up
for hours of
prayer and negotiation.

my eyes open wide,
as open eyes look back
at me.
I see you.

Some poems from

MISTY DARKNESS
A BOOK OF POETRY

HARKI DHILLON

Available from amazon.com

Torment

Let the sun scorch my skin
so it feels cool
after your touch.
Let the snowfall
be heavy and silent
as it drifts onto
my upturned face
so I can focus on your essence
deep within me.
Let the monsoon rains
drench the land
and bring the fresh damp smell
of steaming earth
to my nostrils
as I walk barefoot
in my sodden and dripping clothes.

Darkness in the day
thunder and lightning
all bringing together
the vision
of your dark hair and eyelashes,
your lithe and sinuous form
exposed by your brilliant smile
All sound now drowned
by the beating of my heart.
I stand on the mountain,
the wind whipping
my clothes, my hair, my skin,
my eyes.
Cleansing tears flow freely,
Your memory lifts me higher,
beyond the summit.
I cannot escape your presence
I cannot escape you.

Let me come home
into your arms, your heart,
your being.
Torment me no more.

Enough

Are you in the lagoon
having passed through stormy seas.
Do you feel drained,
with hope a struggling flame
deep within,
to search for happiness,
to search for a kindred soul,

to search for comfort and
companionship
and, maybe love.
To shed the cloak of bitterness
with its tendrils
wrapped around each emotional fiber,
to purge regret
and spring to freedom,
to breathe sweet air
Without the grip of sadness
the crushing force released,
to remember with courage
the moment you cried
Enough.

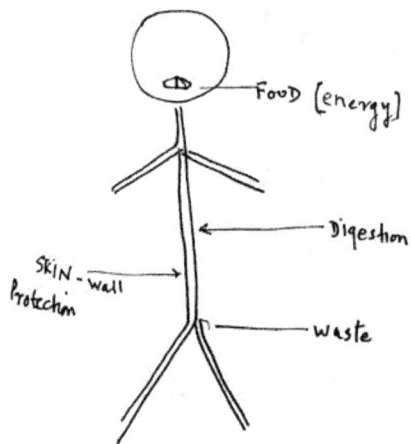

FooD (energy)

Digestion

SKIN - Wall
Protection

Waste

HUMAN
30-40 trillion cells.

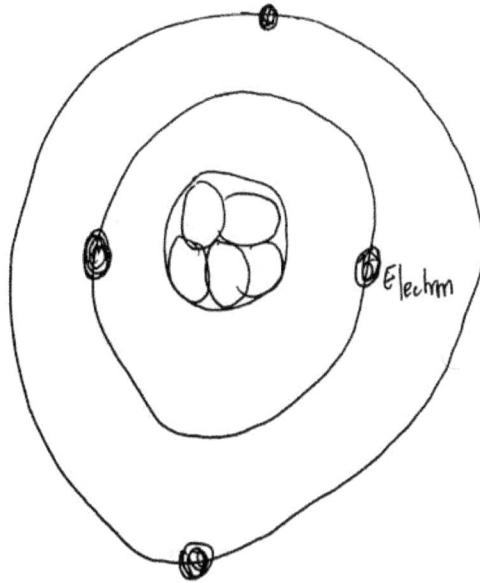

ATOM.

Our atomic Structure is Hydrogen (65%), Oxygen (24%) and Carbon (10%)

www.ingramcontent.com/pod-product-compliance
Lightning Source LLC
LaVergne TN
LVHW061217060426
835508LV00014B/1341